Contents

Glossary

Words in **CAPITALS** are further
explained under 'Words and names'
on pages 46–47.

Anglo-
The Anglo-Saxons used a silver penny, about the size of a modern ten-pence piece, but with a value equal to a modern £20 note. A horse, for example, cost 120 pence and a sheep 4 pence. On one side was the king's head and his name; on the other side was a cross. Because pennies were such large amounts of money, halfpennies and farthings were made towards the end of Anglo-Saxon times by cutting an existing penny into halves or quarters.

The Anglo-Saxons

This book is about Anglo-Saxons – a people who lived over a thousand years ago. For about five hundred years, the Anglo-Saxons developed a way of life that has helped shape the way we live today.

The **ANGLO-SAXONS** were people from north-western Europe who began to invade England while the **ROMANS** were still in control, over 1,500 years ago.

During the following centuries, they settled and their descendants ruled for about five hundred years (a hundred years longer than the Romans). However, unlike the Romans, the Anglo-Saxons never 'went home'; many people living in Britain today have Anglo-Saxon **ANCESTORS**. The name England even comes from one of the Anglo-Saxon peoples – the **ANGLES**.

On this page you will learn briefly about what happened during Anglo-Saxon times. The rest of the book tells you more.

❶ The Anglo-Saxons were groups of people who came from what is now Denmark, Germany and The Netherlands.

❷ They shared the same kind of language, but they were not a single people like the Romans. Instead, they were more like **TRIBES**, each ruled by strong **WARRIORS** – called **WAR LORDS**.

❸ The first Anglo-Saxons raided the shores of south and east England in the fourth century AD, but they were beaten back by the Romans.

❹ But once the Romans left Britain, the **BRITISH** invited Anglo-Saxon tribes to help keep out invaders from Scotland and Ireland. In return, they offered money and land.

❺ It was not long before the Anglo-Saxons took over most of England

Anglo-Saxon
raiders and settlers

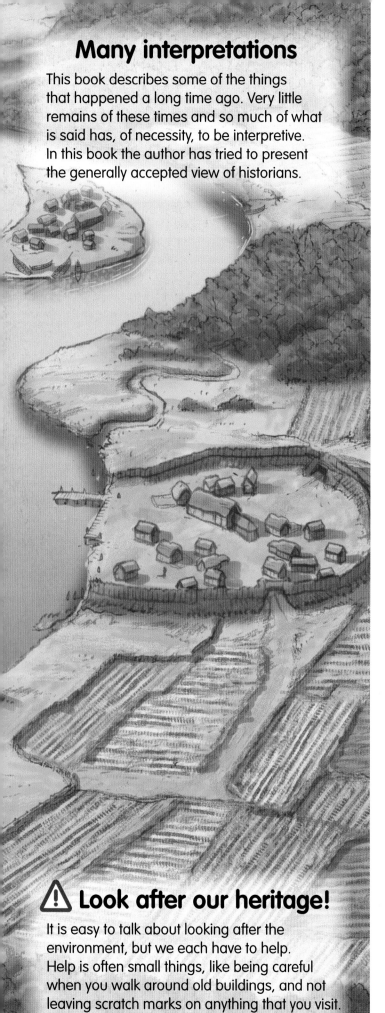

Many interpretations

This book describes some of the things that happened a long time ago. Very little remains of these times and so much of what is said has, of necessity, to be interpretive. In this book the author has tried to present the generally accepted view of historians.

⚠ Look after our heritage!

It is easy to talk about looking after the environment, but we each have to help. Help is often small things, like being careful when you walk around old buildings, and not leaving scratch marks on anything that you visit. It doesn't take a lot of effort – just attitude.

⬭ Curriculum Visions ⬭

Curriculum Visions is a registered trademark of Atlantic Europe Publishing Company Ltd.

There's more on-line

There's more about other great Curriculum Visions packs and a wealth of supporting information available at our dedicated web site. Visit:

⬭ www.CurriculumVisions.com ⬭

 Atlantic Europe Publishing

First published in 2005 by
Atlantic Europe Publishing Company Ltd.
Copyright © 2005
Atlantic Europe Publishing Company Ltd.

Author
Brian Knapp, BSc, PhD

Editor
Robert Anderson, BA, PGCE

Art Director
Duncan McCrae, BSc

Designed and produced by
EARTHSCAPE EDITIONS

Senior Designer
Adele Humphries, BA, PGCE

Printed in China by
WKT Company Ltd

Anglo-Saxon raiders and settlers – *Curriculum Visions*
A CIP record for this book is available from the British Library

Paperback ISBN 1 86214 433 8
Hardback ISBN 1 86214 435 4

Illustrations (c=centre t=top b=bottom l=left r=right)
Mark Stacey cover, 1, 2, 3, 4–5, 6, 8–9, 14, 22–23, 24–25, 28–29, 30–31, 32–33, 37, 39; *David Woodroffe* pages 3tr, 7, 11, 34tr, 35tl, 38.

Picture credits
All photographs are from the Earthscape Editions photolibrary except the following: (c=centre t=top b=bottom l=left r=right) *The British Library* page 34; *The British Museum* pages 13, 16, 17, 18, 20, 21; *The Granger Collection, New York* pages 15, 19t, 22tl, 40, 41, 42, 43tr, 43b.

This product is manufactured from sustainable managed forests. For every tree cut down at least one more is planted.

and built villages, giving them the names we still use today. In this way, they stopped being invaders and became settlers.

6 Anglo-Saxon England became divided into several kingdoms. The biggest were **WESSEX**, **MERCIA** and **NORTHUMBRIA**.

7 In the ninth century, Anglo-Saxon England came under attack from **VIKING** raiders from Norway and northern Denmark. Half a century later, these Vikings began to settle, just as the Anglo-Saxons had done.

8 For the next two hundred years, there was a struggle between Vikings and Anglo-Saxons for the lands of England. Each group

controlled about half of the country. Finally, the Anglo-Saxon and Viking parts of England merged and became one kingdom. Sometimes there was an Anglo-Saxon king, and sometimes a Viking one.

9 In 1066, the Anglo-Saxon king of England died and three people fought for the crown: Anglo-Saxon Harold from England, Viking Harald Hadrade from Norway and **NORMAN** William from Normandy (France). When William won the struggle (and became known as William the Conqueror), he replaced all of the Anglo-Saxon lords with Norman ones and so brought Anglo-Saxon times to an end.

Who were the Anglo-Saxons?

The Anglo-Saxons were tribes from north-western Europe who raided, invaded and then settled England between AD 350 and 1066.

The story of the **ANGLO-SAXONS** begins around the time when the **ROMANS** decided to abandon Britain after 400 years of rule.

Raiders

For many years before they left Britain, the Romans had had to defend the southern and eastern shores from hit-and-run raids by small groups of people from the mainland of Europe.

The raiders included the **ANGLES**, the **SAXONS** and the **JUTES**.

The largest groups were the Angles and Saxons and so we often know them as the Anglo-Saxons. They came from the lands we now call Germany, Denmark and The Netherlands – lands that lie to the east of England, across the North Sea.

The Anglo-Saxons were **PAGAN** peoples and believed in war and battle as a way of gaining wealth and **SLAVES**.

▼ ① Anglo-Saxons raiding the British shores. In the background you can see a villa that has been abandoned by the Romans.

For more on the times leading up to the arrival of the Angles, Saxons and Jutes, see the Curriculum Visions title *The Romans in Britain.*

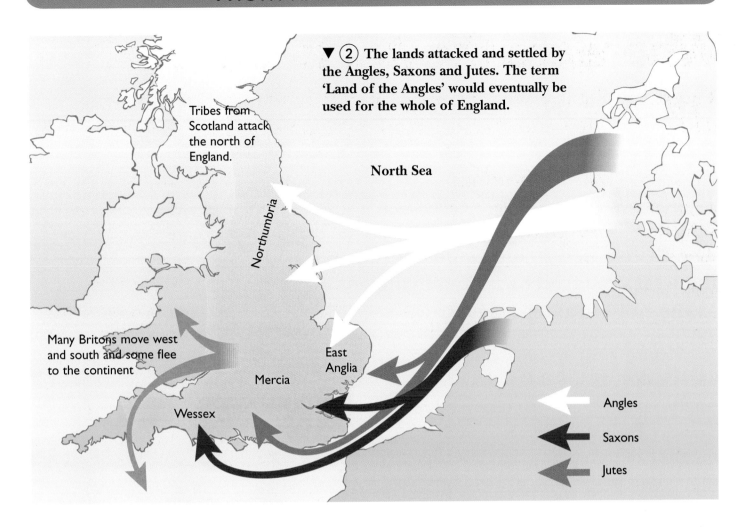

Tribes from Scotland attack the north of England.

North Sea

Northumbria

Many Britons move west and south and some flee to the continent

East Anglia

Mercia

Wessex

▼ ② The lands attacked and settled by the Angles, Saxons and Jutes. The term 'Land of the Angles' would eventually be used for the whole of England.

← Angles

← Saxons

← Jutes

The Romans used armed ships and a line of forts to try to keep the Anglo-Saxons away from England.

Invasion

At the beginning of the fifth century, the Romans left Britain. They had not trained the **BRITISH** to defend themselves, so the people living in what is today England became an easy target for peoples, like the Angles and Saxons, who wanted new lands (picture ①).

It was, however, not just the Anglo-Saxons who saw the British as an easy target. So did the tribes in Scotland. The British quickly realised that, to survive, they would need help.

As it happened, the Romans had used Saxon troops from Germany to help them defend the Roman empire. So the British naturally turned to them for help in protecting their northern border.

The Saxons did help repel the people from Scotland, but, having done so, refused to go home. As news of the weakness of the British got back to the Anglian and Saxon homelands, more and more of their people came over and settled in southern Britain (picture ②). It was the beginning of Anglo-Saxon England.

Where did the Anglo-Saxons settle?

The Anglo-Saxons settled in places near to rivers or the sea. The British fled to hilly lands in the west or stayed on, often living as the Anglo-Saxons' slaves.

It was during the second half of the fifth century that more and more Anglo-Saxons arrived to take land for themselves. It is for this reason that the time of the Anglo-Saxons is usually thought of as beginning about AD 450.

The earliest settlements

At this time, most of Britain was still covered in forest. There were perhaps no more than a few hundred thousand people in the whole land (today there are about 50 million). So it was still an easy place for newcomers to find a place to start a village and then turn the surrounding forest into farmland (picture ①). It was, of course, much less work to take over land already cleared by the **BRITISH**.

The newcomers usually settled in places that could easily be reached by boat, such as the east coast of England or along the banks of the big rivers like the Thames and the Humber.

Untouched forest

Water meadows used for grazing animals

Most settlements were small, home to just a **CHIEFTAIN** and a small number of followers. But even so, they had to be places that were easy to defend. An island in a river was a favourite choice. Another popular place was inside a sharp curve, or meander, in a river. A third place was in the angle where two rivers met.

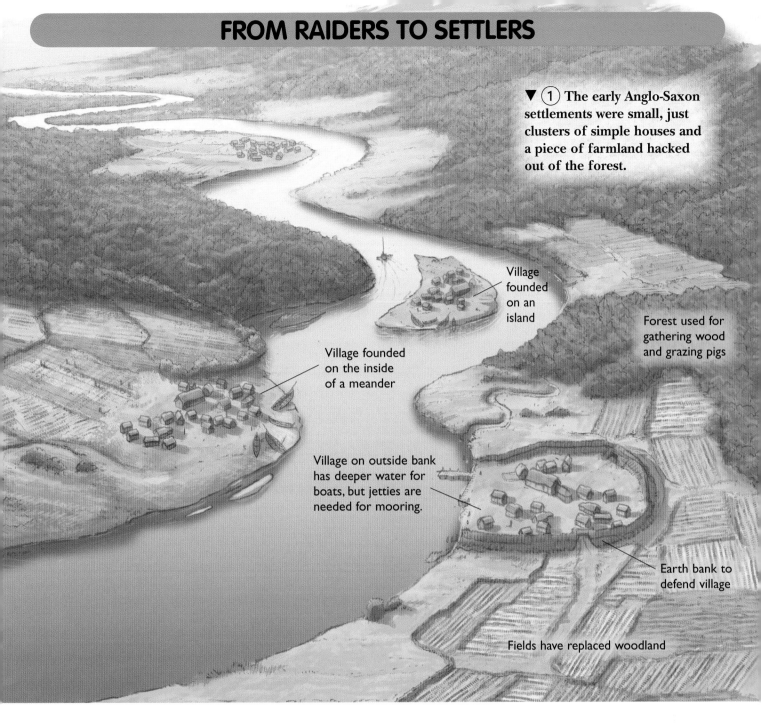

▼ ① The early Anglo-Saxon settlements were small, just clusters of simple houses and a piece of farmland hacked out of the forest.

Village founded on an island

Forest used for gathering wood and grazing pigs

Village founded on the inside of a meander

Village on outside bank has deeper water for boats, but jetties are needed for mooring.

Earth bank to defend village

Fields have replaced woodland

What happened to the British?

As the Anglo-Saxons invaded, some of the British fled westward, to hilly or remote lands such as present day Wales and Cornwall. Many, however, lived alongside the newcomers. We know this because of evidence from **ARCHAEOLOGY**. The British were Christians. They did not bury treasures with their dead. The early Anglo-Saxons were **PAGANS**, and they buried many treasures with their dead.

Many early Anglo-Saxon cemeteries have been found that contain the graves of people buried without treasures. This tells us that Christian British sometimes lived alongside pagan Anglo-Saxons. The British may often have been beaten in battle by the Anglo-Saxons and then lived as **SLAVES**, as was the custom of the time.

Our Anglo-Saxon place names

The Anglo-Saxons named many of the places where we now live. The words they used can tell us what the places were once like or the name of the local leader.

The British people had already named hills, rivers and other parts of the landscape. Some of these names have survived in more remote places which were not taken over by the Anglo-Saxons. Many more place names, however, have their origins in Anglo-Saxon times (pictures ①, ② and ③).

Names that tell of tribes

The first Anglo-Saxon villages were often named after the **CHIEFTAIN** who won the land. This made it clear to which **TRIBE** the village belonged.

These places often have the letters 'ing' or 'folk' somewhere in the name, often at the end. Both these words mean 'people'. The first part of the place name will probably be the name of the local chieftain. For example, Reading means 'Redda's people' and Hastings, 'Haesta's people'.

Names that tell of the landscape

Most later villages were named after a feature of their surroundings rather than the name of a chieftain (pictures ① and ②).

▲ ① Like many Anglo-Saxon settlements, Henley in Oxfordshire was founded next to a river. Its name means a 'high clearing in a forest'.

HENLEY ON THAMES

WARNING
ENGINE DRIVERS MUST ON
TAKE ONE LOADED TRUCK
ONE TIME OVER THIS BRIDG
OWNERS AND DRIVERS AR
RESPONSIBLE FOR DAMAGE

For example, Oxford got its name because it was a place where oxen were driven across a ford in a river.

Places named after gods

Other places were named after pagan gods. For example, the town of Wednesfield in the West Midlands was named in honour of the god Woden, while Tuesley in Surrey was named after the god Tiw.

Note: The Viking peoples also named the places which they founded. These are described in the companion book *Viking raiders and settlers*.

▼ ③ Can you work out where the places on this map got their names?

▼ ② Below are some of the Anglo-Saxon words that occur in modern place names. Can you think of place names close to you that include these words?

Anglo-Saxon	Meaning	Example of place name
barrow	wood	Barrow-in-Furness
bury	fortified place	Banbury
ham	village	Wolsingham
hurst	wooden hill	Chistlehurst
leigh/lee/ley	forest clearing	Henley
mer/mar/mere	lake	Cromer
port	market town	Bridport
stead/sted	place	Stanstead
stow/stowe	meeting place	Stowmarket
ton/tun	enclosed village	Tonbridge
wick/wich	farm	Norwich

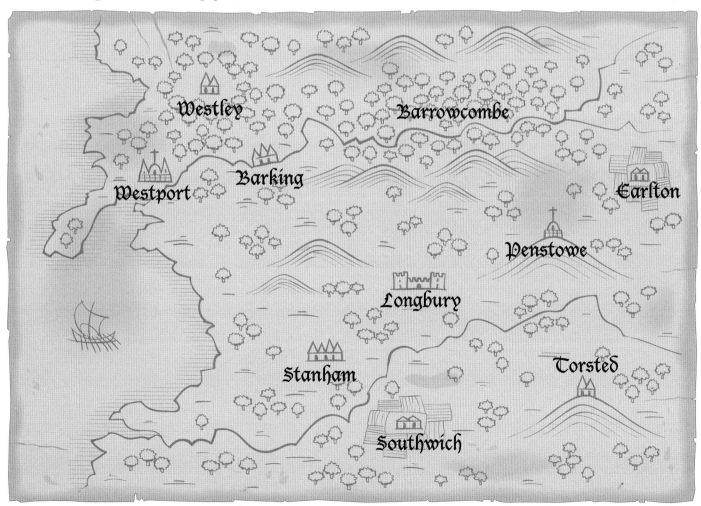

Westley

Barrowcombe

Barking

Westport

Earlton

Penstowe

Longbury

Stanham

Torsted

Southwich

From pagans to Christians

The early Anglo-Saxons were pagans but, as time passed, gradually converted to Christianity. However, many pagan customs survived.

▲ (1) Part of an early Anglo-Saxon cross from Escomb, County Durham.

When the Christian missionaries first converted the Anglo-Saxons, they could not build churches immediately. Instead, they built brightly painted stone crosses, usually at the places where the pagan temples had stood. In time, a wooden church was built next to the cross (see pages 26 and 27).

Where do we come from? What made the Earth, the sky and the food we eat? These were the sorts of questions the Anglo-Saxons asked themselves.

The Anglo-Saxons came up with an answer: they were controlled by superhuman people – gods and goddesses. They also believed that they were directly descended from their gods. The gods included: Woden, the god of war and widsom; Frigg, the goddess of love; Thunor, the god of thunder; and Tiw, another god of battle. They were similar to the gods of the Vikings.

Certain days of the week are named after early Anglo-Saxon gods (and were also used, with slight changes of name, by the pagan Vikings, who had a similar language). Tuesday is named after Tiw, Wednesday after Woden, Thursday after Thunor and Friday after Frigg.

Anglo-Saxons became **WARRIORS** because to die in battle was a glorious death and meant that you could enter **VALHALLA**, a banqueting hall ruled over by Woden.

Conversion

In AD 597 the **POPE** in Rome sent a **MISSIONARY**, St Augustine, to England to convert the Anglo-Saxons to Christianity (picture ①).

▼ ② This beautifully carved Anglo-Saxon box was made out of whalebone in the early eighth century. It is known as the Franks Casket. The carvings show how Christian and pagan beliefs existed side by side in Anglo-Saxon times. One of the carvings shows the pagan legend of Weland the Smith, while another depicts the three wise men visiting the newborn Christ.

Christians believed in peace and everlasting life, and did not consider dying in battle glorious. As Anglo-Saxons were converted from pagan beliefs to Christian ones, they changed their way of life and became less warlike.

The pope gave orders that pagan temples should be converted into Christian ones, and that pagan celebrations should also be made into Christian ones. In this way, pagan celebrations and places of worship became a fixed part of the Christian way of life (picture ②).

▼ ① During Anglo-Saxon times, monks produced many written documents. They were all religious works, and great care was taken in their preparation. Many are brightly coloured and are called illuminated manuscripts.

Learning about the early Anglo-Saxons from records

We can find out important things about the early Anglo-Saxons from the people who wrote down their history.

Written records are one important way in which we can learn about the past. Another source is what we find when we dig up, or excavate, a place where people once lived. We call this ARCHAEOLOGY.

Anglo-Saxon history

It is impossible to make an accurate account of what went on in the early years of the Anglo-Saxon raids and invasions. It was a time of war and struggle. There were few people who could write and little chance to make good-quality buildings that lasted.

So what we know about the early years comes almost entirely from a few accounts written much later in Anglo-Saxon times and from a tiny number of sites where Anglo-Saxon remains have been found (see pages 16 to 23).

▲ ② An illuminated (decorated) page from Bede's *The Ecclesiastical History of the English People*.

The Ecclesiastical History of the English People

This is part of what Bede wrote, some 300 years after the Anglo-Saxons arrived. It tells of the way the Anglo-Saxons were first invited to Britain to help defend against the peoples in the north. It has been changed from Latin into modern English.

"Then the nations of the Angles, or Saxons, being invited by the (British) king, arrived in Britain with three longships, and were given a place to stay in the eastern part of the island. At first they appeared to be fighting for the British but their real intentions were to enslave them. Accordingly they fought against the enemy from the north and were victorious. When this was known in their own country, and also the fertility of the country, and the cowardice of the Britons, more Angles and Saxons were quickly sent over to Britain.

"…In a short time, swarms of the aforesaid nations came over into the island, and they began to increase so much, that they became terrible to the natives themselves who had invited them.

"…Others, continuing in their own country, led a miserable life among the woods, rocks and mountains, with scarcely enough food to support life, and expecting every moment to be their last."

All of the accounts were written by monks and other men of the church. At this time, they were usually the only people who could read and write (picture ①).

The Venerable Bede

One of the most important accounts was written by the Venerable **BEDE**, a priest who lived in the late seventh and early eighth centuries. His account is known as *The Ecclesiastical History of the English People* and was written in **LATIN**. Bede's book tells the history of Britain from the Roman invasion to the arrival of St Augustine in AD 597. In writing his history, Bede used not only earlier written records but also the spoken stories passed down from generation to generation. Other important works include the **LINDISFARNE GOSPELS** and the **ANGLO-SAXON CHRONICLES** (diary).

Learning about the Anglo-Saxons from the grave at Sutton Hoo

▼ ① The Sutton Hoo site is near Ipswich in Suffolk.

Sutton Hoo •

Much of what we know about the Anglo-Saxons comes from graves like the one at Sutton Hoo in Suffolk.

The Anglo-Saxons left little that has survived to modern times. But there is one place where archaeologists found spectacular remains in 1939. It is called **SUTTON HOO** in Suffolk (picture ①) and it gives a glimpse of what Anglo-Saxon life was like.

▼ ② This lid was made to cover a leather pouch containing gold coins. It hung by three hinged straps from the waist belt, and was fastened by a gold buckle. The decorations include two identical images of a man standing between two wolves. The wolves may refer to the family name of the king buried at Sutton Hoo – the Wuffingas ('Wolf's people'). They represent strength and courage, qualities that a successful Anglo-Saxon leader had to possess.

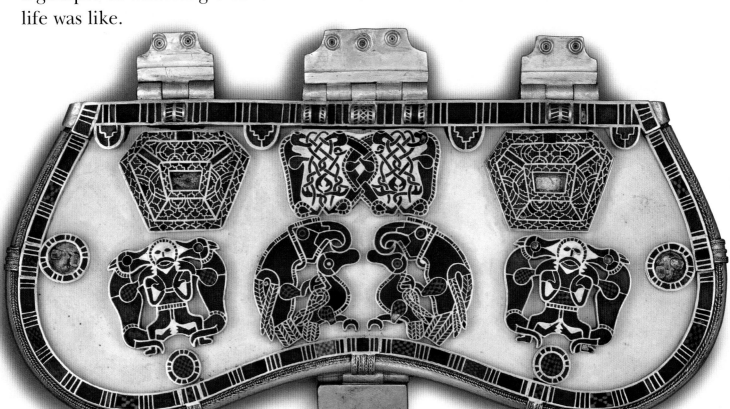

▲ ③ These gold coins were found in the leather purse whose lid is shown on page 16. There were thirty-seven gold coins; three coin-sized blanks and two bars of gold. All the coins were made between AD 575 and AD 620.

The dates of the coins tell us that the burial could not have taken place before 620.

This is a pagan burial, because Christians do not need grave goods. So the king that was buried had not converted to Christianity.

Sutton Hoo burial ship

At Sutton Hoo there is a large mound of earth covering the burial of an important Anglo-Saxon chief, probably King Raedwald who ruled East Anglia in the seventh century. He was buried inside a ship, along with lots of treasures, which the Anglo-Saxons believed he would need in the afterlife.

The ship is huge – around 30 metres from bow to stern and nearly 5 metres at its widest.

The burial

Archaeologists think that the ship was dragged to the top of a cliff from the river below. It was then placed in a trench that had been specially dug for it (see pages 22 and 23).

A hut was built in the middle of the ship and the coffin and treasures (called **GRAVE GOODS**) placed inside it. The ship was then completely covered with a mound of earth.

What the grave goods tell us

The grave goods at Sutton Hoo have survived in good condition. They include ornamental purses (picture ②) and gold coins (picture ③); a battle shield (picture ④, page 18) and gold weapons and **ARMOUR**;

tableware and drinking horns (picture ⑤, page 19). The most astonishing treasure, however, is an iron battle helmet (picture ⑥, page 20 and picture ⑦, page 21).

Some of the grave goods were not made in England but other countries. Some large silver dishes, for example, were made in the Middle East in about AD 500.

▼ ④ The shield found at Sutton Hoo had to be reconstructed (rebuilt). This was because all its wooden and leather parts had rotted away in the ground, leaving only the metal parts intact.

The shield was rebuilt with boards of limewood and covered in cowhide. The remains of the original shield were placed on the new shield to show where they once belonged. You can see a gold-covered bird of prey and a six-winged dragon. These may be symbols of courage.

The iron boss (knob) from the centre of the shield is decorated with pairs of horses. The shield is nearly a metre across.

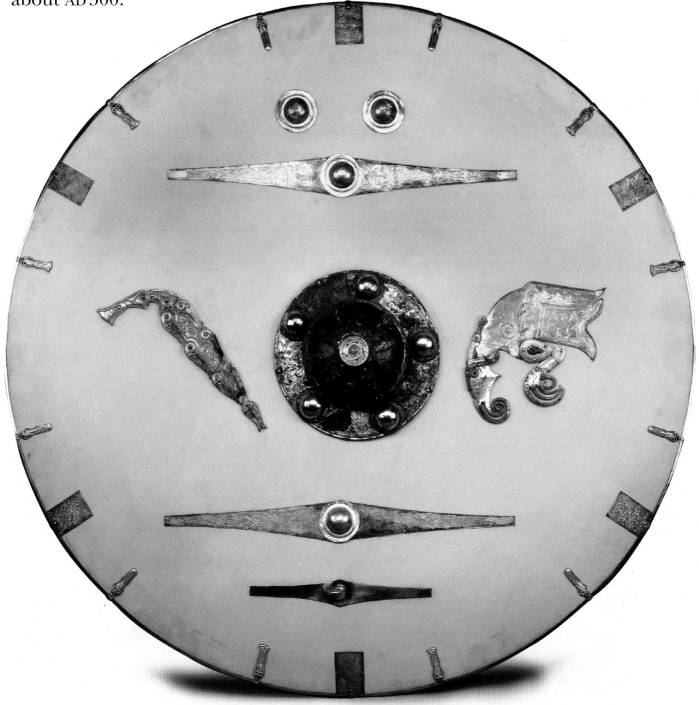

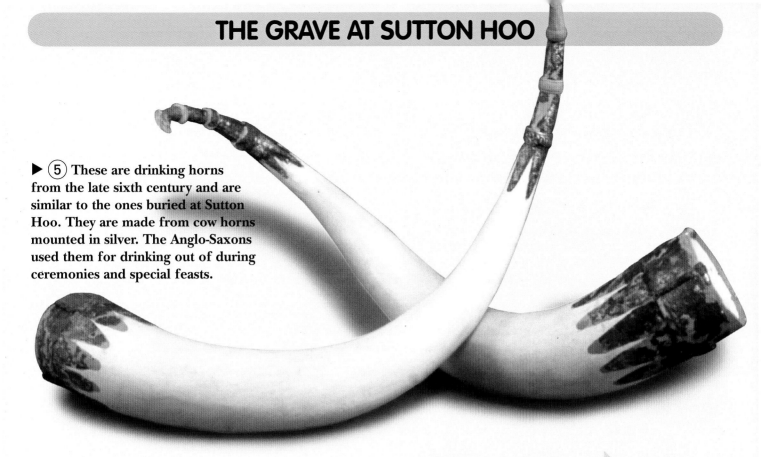

▶ ⑤ These are drinking horns from the late sixth century and are similar to the ones buried at Sutton Hoo. They are made from cow horns mounted in silver. The Anglo-Saxons used them for drinking out of during ceremonies and special feasts.

This tells us that trade between England and the rest of Europe was common in Anglo-Saxon times. The fact that these foreign goods are often much older than the grave tells us that people handed goods down from one generation to the next.

Were all people given ship burials?

Ship burials were reserved for the most powerful people (see pages 22 and 23). So just a few burials were of this kind. Sometimes the burial ships were cast adrift in the sea, sometimes they were buried on land.

Important men, especially if they were warriors, were buried with weapons such as a sword, a spear and a shield. Important women, by contrast, were buried with items such as herbs and spices, which were symbols of healing.

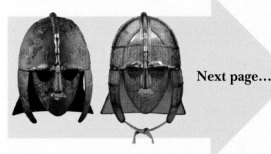

Next page...

▶ ⑥ and ⑦ (pages 20 and 21) The Sutton Hoo helmet. Anglo-Saxons mostly wore leather helmets and only the wealthiest had helmets made of iron. Besides the Sutton Hoo helmet, only three other iron helmets have been found.

Picture ⑥ shows the fragments that archaeologists found at Sutton Hoo. The pieces are set out on a copper-coloured base. Picture ⑦ is a reconstruction based on the fragments.

The helmet was decorated with heroic scenes. The decorations might look like they are made out of gold but are in fact tinned bronze. One scene shows two warriors, wearing horned helmets, holding short swords and spears. The other scene shows a mounted warrior trampling a fallen enemy.

The face-mask has eye-sockets, eyebrows and a nosepiece. The bronze eyebrows are decorated with silver wire and semi-precious stones. Placed against the top of the nose is a gilded dragonhead. The nose and eyebrows make up a great bird with outstretched wings that seems to fly across the helmet, rather like the bird of prey on the shield.

◀ ⑧ This photograph shows the Sutton Hoo site shortly after archaeologists discovered it. The remains of the soil mound can be seen on the right. The pit shows the shape of the ship, whose wood had largely rotted away.

Once the burial services are over, the ship is covered with soil.

Most Anglo-Saxon people were cremated (burnt) after they died, and their remains placed in urns. Grave goods have also been found near urns.

Why do we not find more Anglo-Saxon burials?

Mounds like those of Sutton Hoo were widely known to be the resting places of chiefs and kings. It would also have been known that they contained treasures.

This tempted people to rob the graves of their treasures. As a result, most burial sites are empty.

▼ ⑨ How the Sutton Hoo burial may have happened.

A real ship has been hauled into a trench.

The body of the leader has been laid out and grave goods placed around him.

Weblink: www.CurriculumVisions.com

The Anglo-Saxon village

Anglo-Saxon villages were usually very small and sited close to natural resources that would help the villagers survive.

The first Anglo-Saxon settlements were tiny. But over the centuries they grew larger and became more organised. Nevertheless, even the largest were home to no more than a few hundred people.

So what would an Anglo-Saxon village have been like by the eighth or ninth century? Using evidence that archaeologists have discovered, we can try to reconstruct a typical example (picture ①).

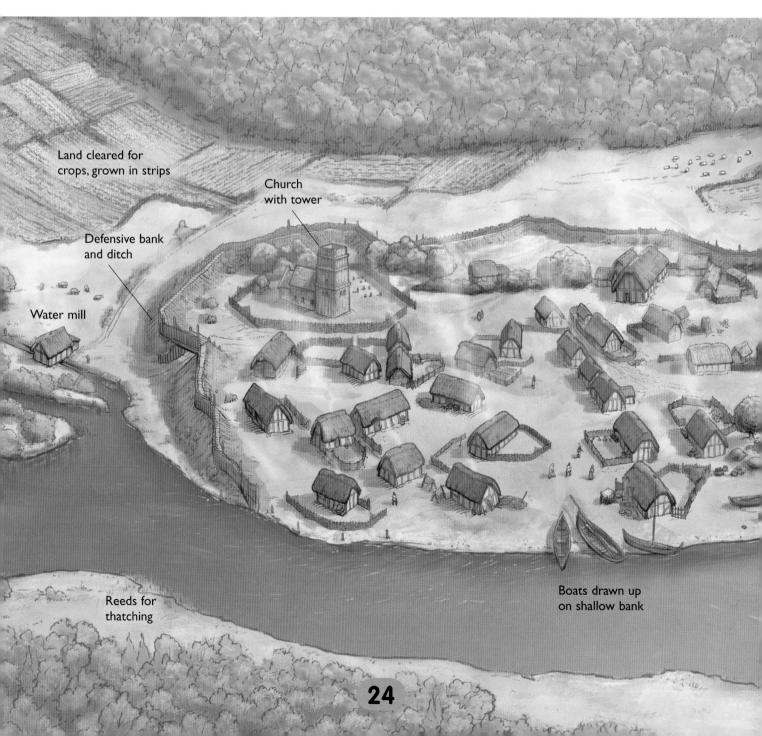

Land cleared for crops, grown in strips

Church with tower

Defensive bank and ditch

Water mill

Reeds for thatching

Boats drawn up on shallow bank

Water, food and fuel

First, let's think about the basics of life. The village people needed water, food, fuel for heating and cooking, and materials for homes and clothes. The village also needed to protect itself.

▼ ① **Here you can see an Anglo-Saxon village in the eighth century. You can see the fences separating the homes, the church and the quayside. Some homes lie along a line that might become a street in time. Others, though, are simply scattered about in no particular pattern.**

Untouched forest

Land cleared for crops, grown in strips

Water meadows for livestock grazing

Navigable river

Water could most easily come from a river or spring. With more effort, it could come from a well. If the village was sited next to a river, however, it was vital to choose a place that did not get flooded.

Food could only come from the nearby land, so most villages were placed near to easily worked fertile soils. Other areas, with heavy clays or acid soils, were left alone.

Everyone used wood for a fuel, and wood, mud, straw, reeds and dung to make buildings. Wood came from a woodland, and reeds (for roof thatching) from marshland by the river. The forest could also serve other important purposes such as a place where pigs could eat.

Getting about and keeping safe

In Anglo-Saxon times most people travelled by boat and lived close to rivers. But being close to a river also meant that you could easily be attacked by raiders.

To help give some protection, an earth bank was often built around the village with stakes driven into the top of it. There might also be a stone watchtower (see page 26), which might be part of a church.

Watchtowers and churches

The Anglo-Saxons built the first churches in England. But they were not just for praying in – they had other purposes, too.

If you look for signs of ancient people in England, you will find the remains of many Roman buildings and even the remains of **HILL FORTS** that were built before the Romans arrived. But you will not find many buildings from Anglo-Saxon times.

The reason for this is that the Anglo-Saxon period was mainly one of great violence and struggle.

Most Anglo-Saxon buildings were built of wood, so when a village was attacked wooden buildings were easily burned to the ground. Over time, too, they would have rotted away, anyway.

But there was one group of buildings that were different. These were the towers and churches.

Towers

The Anglo-Saxons built towers in order to keep watch over the surrounding countryside. No one knew when an enemy might approach. The towers needed to be strong and long-lasting and so were built of stone. These watchtowers could be used like mini-castles to protect villagers from attack,

Tower entrance

▲ ① Towers were often built before the church because they were used as lookouts and defensive buildings. The door to the church at Earls Barton in Northampton is just below the modern clock. It was reached by an outside ladder that could be drawn up if raiders approached. (The battlements at the very top of the tower were added after Anglo-Saxon times.)

and many towers had upper rooms that could only be reached by a ladder. Stones could be thrown down and arrows fired from the top of the tower (picture ①).

Churches

The earliest churches were built of wood, but as the English church grew richer, they were replaced by buildings of stone (pictures ①, ② and ③).

Churches were often built against the watchtowers. This is why, in later centuries, a tower became a typical part of church design.

The wealth of the church was also the reason why, when Vikings raided Anglo-Saxon villages after the ninth century, they made straight for the church. Inside they might find treasures like a gold-covered cross or a jewel-encrusted Bible.

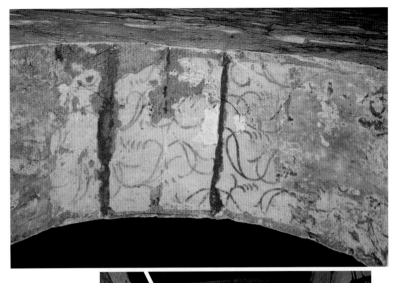

▼ ③ Early Anglo-Saxon churches were meant to serve just a small number of people. This Anglo-Saxon church in Bradford-on-Avon, Wiltshire, is tiny – barely bigger than a modern house.

As the number of people in a village increased, these churches became too small. Many were pulled down and rebuilt on a bigger scale. This is one reason why so few Anglo-Saxon churches survive.

▲ ② The interior of the church at Escomb, County Durham. The church is tall and narrow – a typical Anglo-Saxon design. The walls were painted with bright colours, not white as they are today. The inside of the arch (inset above) still shows how it was decorated over a thousand years ago.

Homes and halls

Most Anglo-Saxons lived in single-roomed huts. Even the wealthiest lived in one-roomed wooden 'hall houses'.

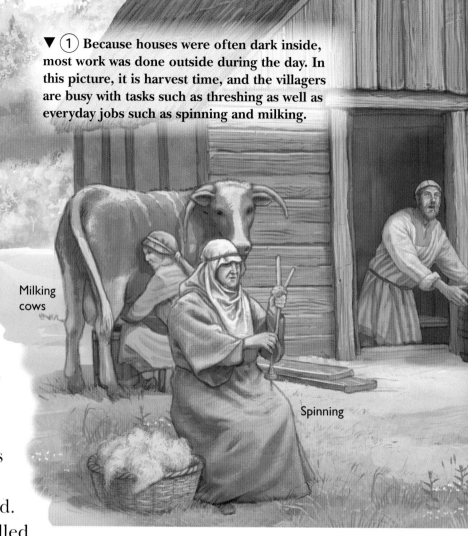

▼ ① Because houses were often dark inside, most work was done outside during the day. In this picture, it is harvest time, and the villagers are busy with tasks such as threshing as well as everyday jobs such as spinning and milking.

Milking cows

Spinning

We can mostly only guess what Anglo-Saxon homes were like because they have all rotted away or been burned down.

However, when the houses were burned down charcoal stumps were left in the ground. If the posts rotted or were pulled up, different soil was put in to fill the holes up. These traces of Anglo-Saxon homes still survive.

Simple houses

Using the pattern of these post holes we know that no one in Anglo-Saxon times lived in the kinds of grand houses that the Romans had known. Instead, they mainly lived in small single-roomed huts perhaps 4 metres long by 3 metres wide. Nobles simply lived in larger wooden huts. We call the larger buildings 'hall houses'.

The spaces between the main posts could be filled with oak planks or with a mesh of twigs (called wattle). This wooden 'shell' was made windproof with a coating of mud, straw and dung (called daub). A very small number of houses were made with stone. It all depended on what was close at hand.

Warm floors

Some Anglo-Saxon homes had a sunken floor which was filled with straw and then covered with planks. This helped keep the house warm in winter and was also somewhere to store things. There was usually a hearth for cooking and heating in the centre of the building placed on stones on the planks.

Fetching water

Threshing corn

Chopping wood

Tending pigs

Roofing

The simple wooden building styles used by the Anglo-Saxons could not support heavy roofs, so most roofs were made from thatch. Thatch was usually made from reeds. If reeds could not be found, turf was used over strips of wood bark. In some cases small slats of wood called shingles were also used. There was no chimney, just a hole in the thatch.

Windows

Ordinary Anglo-Saxons could not get glass. Any window openings would have been covered with parchment – thin animal skins that were otherwise used for writing on. This let a small amount of light in but helped keep out the winter cold.

Furniture

Anglo-Saxon people had little furniture. They may have had earth benches down the sides, covered with wooden planks. They were sat on during the day and used as beds at night. The table would have been a plank of wood on tressles together with simple wooden stools. There would also probably have been a chest with a lock, and a loom for weaving.

Weblink: www.CurriculumVisions.com

Food and drink

Food was fairly basic and often difficult to find if the harvest had been poor.

If you were an Anglo-Saxon, you would not be able to pop down to the supermarket and select foods from all over the world, as we do today, nor store them in a freezer. You ate what you grew and you stored only those things that would last through the winter.

Cereals and vegetables

The Anglo-Saxons grew cereals such as wheat, rye, oats and barley. Wheat was the most difficult to grow and needed fertile fields. So most people grew rye, which they made into a dark, heavy bread. Only the rich ate wheat bread.

Nearly all food was boiled in a cauldron over an open fire in the middle of the house. It was eaten as a kind of stew. Only bread was baked in clay ovens.

Water for cooking

Beer for drinking

Chopped wood from local forests.

When harvests were poor, people had to add ground acorns to the corn, then grind it all into a flour.

Most river water was polluted and unsafe to drink. So barley was used to make weak beer, which was drunk instead of water. Wine imported from the Mediterranean was drunk by those who could afford it.

Common vegetables included carrots, parsnips, cabbages, peas, beans and onions. People also grew some herbs, such as thyme and rosemary. The rich could pay for spices such as pepper, imported from distant lands.

Fruits included apples, cherries and plums. Honey was the only sweetener known at that time.

Most people ate and drank mainly from wooden or clay platters, mugs and bowls. They used their fingers to eat with, but knives were used for cutting meat and spoons for eating soup. Only the very wealthy used drinking horns for wine.

Grinding corn using a quern made of two rough stones.

Fish and meat

Most Anglo-Saxons were vegetarians for the simple reason that they could not get meat very often. Only a few were wealthy enough to pay for the slaughter of an animal.

Pigs were the only animals reared just for their meat. Every other kind of animal served other purposes and were killed only when they became old or ill. Sheep were used for wool. Cows were used for milk and, when they were old, for hides, meat and glue. All animal fat was valuable for making oil for lamps and tallow candles.

Wild animals such as deer and wild boar were still common and could be hunted in the forests – but only if you were the landowner.

It was also possible to catch eel, perch and pike from rivers. Some sea fish, such as herring, were also eaten.

Preserving food

To make meat and fish last through the year, they were dried and salted or pickled. Some was also cured by smoking (kippers, for example, are smoked herring). Milk was made into cheese – a good way of preserving milk over the winter.

◄ ① Most cooking was done inside the house. Everything had to be done by hand. The room would have been smoky as there is no chimney over the fire. Look at this picture and the one on the previous page to get an idea of village life.

Weblink: www.CurriculumVisions.com

Rich and poor

Anglo-Saxon society was made up of rich and poor, of freemen and slaves.

What was it like to live in Anglo-Saxon times? Was everyone equal, or were some more powerful than others?

The Anglo-Saxons lived in warlike times. The stronger and more ruthless you were, the better off and more powerful you became. It was a world dominated by a very few rich people; the majority were pitifully poor.

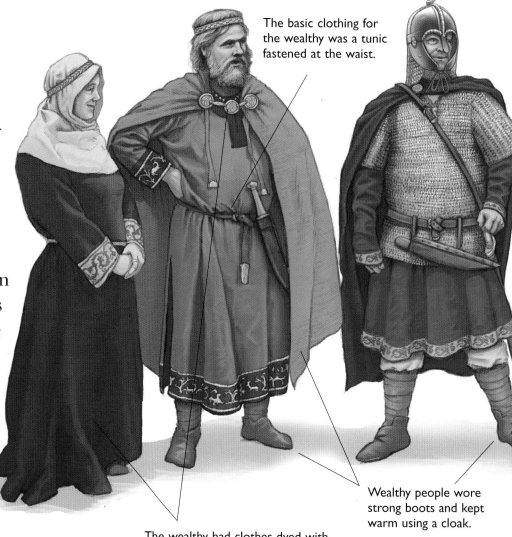

The basic clothing for the wealthy was a tunic fastened at the waist.

The wealthy had clothes dyed with bright colours and fastened with expensive brooches.

Wealthy people wore strong boots and kept warm using a cloak.

The king

It was also a world ruled by men, with a king at the top. The king was a **WAR LORD**. His job was to provide opportunities for plunder and glory for his followers. This was how he paid them for their loyalty. If he did not, then he could expect to be murdered and a stronger person take his place. The king was chosen by a council of leading nobles and bishops. This was called the **WITAN**.

Freemen

Below the king, there were many kinds of **FREEMEN**. If you had more than five **HIDES** of land you were a **THANE**. Thanes were noblemen. They made up the king's bodyguard, and many were full-time warriors.

The most senior nobles were the **EOLDERMEN**, later called eorls (earls), who owned large areas of land. The eolderman also ruled **SHIRES** (counties) or parts of shires called **HUNDREDS**.

The majority of freemen in Anglo-Saxon England owned much less than five hides of land. These people were called **CEORLS** (pronounced churls), no matter how rich or poor they were. They could work their own land but also had to work for the lord on his estate. They could also be called up to join the **FYRD**, the part-time army.

Slaves

Not everyone was free. The **THRALLS** were **SLAVES**. Slaves were obtained by capturing the people who were defeated in battle. Slaves were used as a cheap way of farming the land.

If you were poor, you might sell a son or daughter into slavery so that someone else would take over the job of feeding them. And if you could not pay your debts, you would be made a slave until you had paid off your debts.

Slaves might have children, and in this case the children would also be slaves. People could also be bought out of slavery.

Thanes carried a long spear and a round shield of wood covered with leather. They would only own a sword if they were a warrior.

All poorer people wore a robe of wool or linen, or a tunic gathered at the waist, hose (tight trousers) and soft shoes.

Everyone wore good-luck charms.

The headdress worn by poor people was a kind of hood.

King Offa of Mercia

There were many kings during Anglo-Saxon times. This was because you only remained king for as long as you could beat your enemies.

◀ ① Offa's silver penny.

Today we are used to kings and queens staying on the throne for many years. But in Anglo-Saxon times it was very different.

Battling to stay king

Kings went to war to get treasure, or bounty. Much of this bounty was owed to the people who fought with the king. It was their wages.

So a king could not remain peaceful. He had to fight and keep fighting in order to pay his supporters. When he was no longer able to win battles, his chances of staying alive were small.

This is why Anglo-Saxon times were so violent. King Raedwald of East Anglia (see page 17), for example, must have been a strong king for his followers to give him such a grand burial at Sutton Hoo.

Here we look at the life of another strong king – OFFA of Mercia (pictures ① and ②).

▲ ② Offa getting ready for battle (from a manuscript).

On pages 36 and 37 we look at King Alfred of Wessex, who battled against the Vikings and on pages 40 to 43 you will find out about King Harold who was defeated by William the Conqueror in 1066.

King Offa

King Offa was king of Mercia (the lands we now call the English midlands) between 758 and 796.

To be king for nearly forty years, he must have been a powerful man and a successful warrior.

Offa's Dyke

Offa's Dyke was by far the largest structure built in Anglo-Saxon times. Some people have said the effort needed to build this dyke was as much as building one of the giant pyramids in ancient Egypt.

Offa did not build in stone. Instead, he had a 128-kilometre-long ditch cut into the land, running in a rough line from north to south.

Using earth from the ditch, he also made a bank, or dyke. On top of this he may have put stakes to make it easier to defend.

When it was built, the dyke may have been over 8 metres high. It is still nearly this height in a few places, but for most of its length it is much lower. Nevertheless, it is still a major landmark.

Offa went on campaigns to defeat the kings of Sussex, Anglia and Wessex. He then called himself 'King of the English'.

King Offa was continually faced with attacks on his western borders, from **BRITISH** people in what we now call Wales.

King Offa wanted to fix the boundary, so that it was clear when the Welsh had invaded Mercian land. So he organised the building of one of the biggest earthworks in history. It is now called Offa's Dyke (picture ②).

Did the dyke work?

We cannot be sure how useful the dyke proved to be, but it probably served one long-lasting purpose. It set a boundary for the British people, making them feel that they had something in common. So, in this sense, it probably laid the foundation for the Welsh nation.

But it was only Offa's strength that kept Mercia powerful and wealthy. When Offa died, wars broke out to win control of Mercia. In the 820s, Egbert, king of Wessex, captured the south-east of England from Mercia. Then the Vikings attacked along the east coast, and much of Mercia was lost.

▶▼ ② Offa's Dyke near Clun, Shropshire.

King Alfred resists the Vikings

Alfred was the only king to hold out against the Viking invasion. But even he was only able to hold on to half of England.

In the ninth century, the Anglo-Saxon rule of England faced its most severe challenge. The shores of England were being attacked by **VIKINGS**. An important source for the history of this time is the **ANGLO-SAXON CHRONICLES**.

Viking raids

The Vikings raided the coast in just the same way that the Anglo-Saxons had raided the coast some four centuries earlier (picture ②).

For half a century, they raided and then they invaded. They quickly overwhelmed the people along the eastern coast.

They succeeded because they were better at fighting than the Anglo-Saxons. It was also impossible for the defenders to know where they were going to attack and so muster (gather) an army to beat them.

The Danes beat Alfred

The strongest of the Anglo-Saxon kings in this age was King **ALFRED** (picture ①). His kingdom, **WESSEX**, lay in the south-west of England. He was king between 871 and 900.

The Danish Vikings brought over a large army led by King Guthrum. Guthrum knew he had to defeat Alfred if he was to get control of the country. So Guthrum's army attacked King Alfred's **FYRD** of part-time soldiers, forcing him to flee with a small band of men to marshes in Somerset.

◀ ① **This statue of Alfred stands in Winchester.**

▼ ② Vikings raiding the eastern coast of Anglo-Saxon England.

For more on Viking raids see the Curriculum Visions title *Viking raiders and settlers.*

Alfred regains his lands

Alfred, however, was not defeated. He, in turn, made many hit-and-run raids on the Danes. At the same time, he gradually mustered a strong army.

In 878, Alfred struck back and defeated the Danes at the Battle of Edington.

After the battle, Alfred, now called Alfred the Great, regained the kingdom of Wessex.

Alfred's fame among the English was so great that a Welsh monk named Asser wrote his biography (life story). This is also an important record of the history of the times (see extract opposite).

In his biography of King Alfred, Asser wrote about the Battle of Edington. He uses the word 'pagans' to mean the Vikings.

"King Alfred came to a place called Edington, and with a close shield wall fought fiercely against the whole army of the pagans; his attack was long and spirited, and finally by divine aid he triumphed and overthrew the pagans with a very great slaughter.

"He pursued them, killing them as they fled up to the stronghold, where he seized all that he found outside – men, horses and cattle – slaying the men at once; and before the gates of the pagan fortress he boldly encamped with his whole army.

"And when he had stayed there fourteen days and the pagans had known the horrors of famine, cold, fear, and at last of despair, they sought a peace by which the king was to take from them as many named hostages as he wished while he gave none to them…

"When the king heard their message he was moved to pity, and of his own accord received from them such designated hostages as he wished. In addition to this, after the hostages were taken, the pagans took oath that they would most speedily leave his kingdom…"

Alfred makes Wessex safe

Alfred did not want to lose land to the Viking invaders again, so he set up a network of forts known as burhs. Many burhs developed into towns.

What would you do if you were threatened by invaders who had captured half of your country? This is what King Alfred had to ask himself after his successful battle with the Vikings at Edington (page 37). He had only won a battle; he had not captured the whole country. The Vikings still controlled the east of England, an area that became known as the **DANELAW**.

◀ ① This map shows the three main kingdoms of Anglo-Saxon England – Wessex, Mercia and Northumbria. It also shows the lands taken away from the Anglo-Saxons in the tenth century by the Danish Vikings – the Danelaw.

that Romans had fortified, because they already had walls (for example Gloucester).

Under Alfred's rule no place in Wessex was more than 30 kilometres from a burh. This meant that in times of trouble, it was relatively easy to flee to safety.

The founding of burhs

Alfred decided that the best thing to do was to provide some safe places that his people could retreat to and defend if they were attacked.

The fortified centres were called **BURHS**. Many of them were at places of special importance, such as at fords across rivers (for example Wallingford, Oxfordshire) or by coastal estuaries where the Vikings were likely to attack (for example Wareham, Dorset) (picture ①). Others used the places

What burhs were like

A burh was a fort with earth walls, or dykes, with wooden stakes on top (picture ②). Many places fortified from this time have names that end in -bury (for example Glastonbury).

From fort to town

Burhs were built at places that were easy for people to get to. So in times of peace they were also good places for merchants to live and trade their goods.

In exchange, merchants were required to help to defend the burh. The rule was that one man had to be supplied to defend the equivalent of each metre of wall.

Many other developments followed. For example, because burhs were safe they also became places where coins were minted. So, step by step, burhs quickly became prosperous towns.

As it turned out, the burhs were never needed for defence and instead became the most prosperous Anglo-Saxon towns. As Alfred and his descendants gradually took back parts of the Danelaw, they built new burhs in the recaptured lands, often at ports. Many of these have names ending in -wic or -wich – as, for example Norwich, Ipswich and Aldwych (the Saxon part of London).

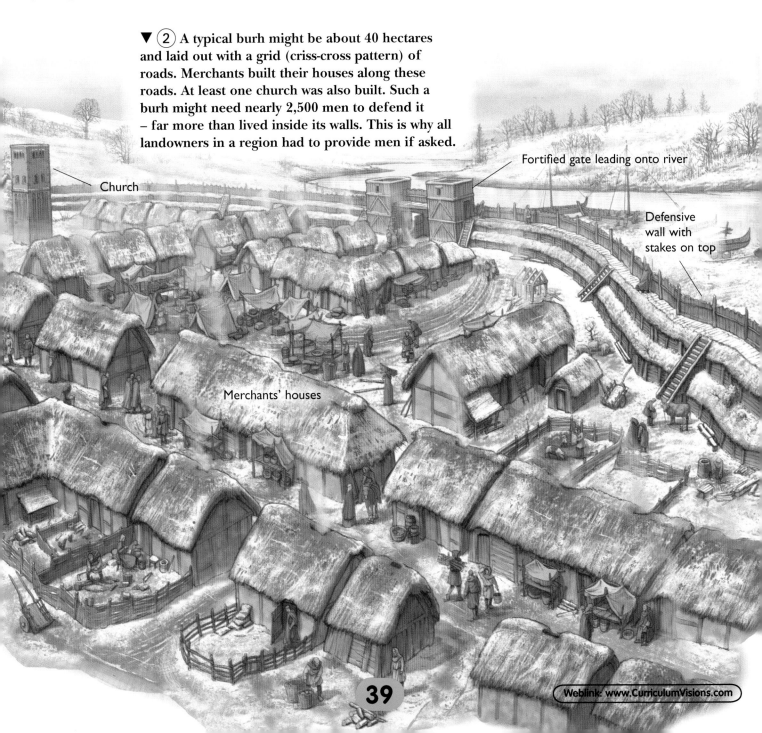

▼ ② A typical burh might be about 40 hectares and laid out with a grid (criss-cross pattern) of roads. Merchants built their houses along these roads. At least one church was also built. Such a burh might need nearly 2,500 men to defend it – far more than lived inside its walls. This is why all landowners in a region had to provide men if asked.

Church

Fortified gate leading onto river

Defensive wall with stakes on top

Merchants' houses

1066: The end of Anglo-Saxon times

The Anglo-Saxons ruled England for over 500 years. But in 1066 the Anglo-Saxon age came to an end with the Battle of Hastings.

Here is the story of the end of Anglo-Saxon times. As it happens, it is also the story of the end of Viking times, because, curiously, they both happened within a week of one another.

The Bayeux Tapestry

Many of the events leading up to the Battle of Hastings, as well as the battle itself, are depicted in the Bayeux Tapestry. The tapestry was commissioned (ordered) by a Norman leader and tells the story from the Norman point of view. It is over 70 metres long, and although it is called a tapestry it is in fact an embroidery, stitched in woollen yarns on linen.

Finally, it is the story of how Anglo-Saxon times became **NORMAN** times, and when the great age of castle-building started. Read about this momentous event over the next four pages…

▼ ① **A scene from the Bayeux Tapestry showing King Harold being crowned.**

AD PEVENE SÆ :-

HIC

▲ ② In this section of the Bayeux Tapestry, William is arriving with his fleet. His boat is on the left and has a signal lamp on the mast. William landed at Pevensey, East Sussex.

Keeping your kingdom

Being king of England was no easy matter. There were always people who wanted your crown and were willing to kill for it. The two competing powers were the Anglo-Saxons and the Vikings. Sometimes the Anglo-Saxons ruled, sometimes the Vikings. It all depended who was the most powerful and ruthless at the time.

King Harold II

This story starts forty four years before the **BATTLE OF HASTINGS**, when, in 1022 Earl Harold Godwinsson was born. By 1042, when Edward the Confessor became king, Harold had made himself the most powerful man in England.

But Edward's main advisers came from Normandy in France. This is where Duke William ruled.

Harold is crowned

Edward did not have a son and so, when he became ill, there was great competition to succeed him. There was Harold, of course, but there were two others who had a claim on the throne: Harald Hadrade, a Viking from Norway and William, Duke of Normandy. It would be a battle of strength to see who would be king.

Harold claimed that Edward promised him the throne just before he died on 5 January 1066. On 6 January 1066, the parliament agreed and made Harold king (picture ①).

Harold waits for attacks

Harold knew that Harald and William would try to get the throne.

He was most worried about William of Normandy, so he kept his army in the south of England. But on the 8th of September, Harald Hadrade sailed from Norway and attacked York, in northern England

Harold then famously said: "I will give Harald just six feet of English soil; or, since they say he is a tall man, I will give him seven feet!", meaning just enough room for a grave.

Harold rushed north with his army and on the 25th of September he defeated the Vikings, killing most of them. No more than 25 of 300 Viking ships returned to Norway.

▼ ③ This section of the Bayeux Tapestry shows the early stages of the Battle of Hastings. Norman horsemen are attacking the shield wall of Harold. Large numbers of dead are shown along the bottom of the tapestry.

William lands

It was bad luck for Harold that this was also the moment William sailed from Normandy. He arrived on England's south coast with 700 ships (picture ②, page 41). So Harold now had to rush back south.

Harold's army was tired from its battle with the Vikings, and they had also had to march an enormous distance. William's men, on the other hand, were fresh and ready for battle.

The Battle of Hastings

The two armies met near Hastings. Harold gathered his men on a hill surrounded by marshes. He quickly ordered the building of a ditch and bank to make his position even stronger. Harold's men then protected themselves with shields

and held huge battle-axes. They were so well protected that neither William's archers nor horsemen could defeat them (picture ③).

But Harold's men did not follow orders and when the Normans fell back, Harold's men charged after them. This opened up a gap in Harold's defences and gave William the chance to attack again.

Before attacking, William told his archers to fire into the air, over the Anglo-Saxon shields. As the arrows came down, legend tells how one arrow struck Harold in the eye, fatally wounding him (picture ④). More likely, however, he was simply hacked to death in the final battle.

William won the battle and the Normans took control (picture ⑤). The Anglo-Saxon age was over. It was 14 October 1066.

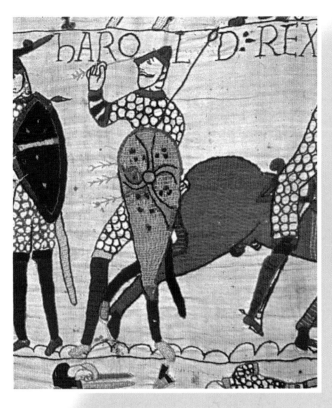

▲ ④ Harold, indicated by the words "Harold Rex" (rex means "king" in Latin), is hit in the eye by an arrow.

▼ ⑤ This part of the Bayeux Tapestry shows the end of the Battle of Hastings. The shield wall is broken and the Anglo-Saxon army is wiped out. William is victorious.

An Anglo-Saxon time line

350 Anglo-Saxons raid English shores and are beaten back by the Romans.

410 Romans leave England, and its shores are unprotected.

450 Traditional date for the arrival of the first Anglo-Saxons in Britain. During the following hundred years, more Anglo-Saxons settle.

597 Christian missionaries, led by St Augustine, arrive in Kent. King Aethelberht of Kent is converted to Christianity.

616 Aethelberht of Kent dies and paganism returns.

616 Raedwald of the East Angles (see page 17) kills Aethelfrith of Northumbria.

758 Offa becomes king of Mercia.

760 By this date, Offa is building a great dyke to protect Mercia from the Welsh.

764 Offa takes direct control of Kent.

771 Offa conquers Sussex.

776 Battle of Otford – Offa of Mercia loses control of Kent until 784/5.

778 Offa raids Dyfed in Wales.

779 Battle of Bensington – Offa of Mercia defeats Cynewulf of Wessex.

784 Offa raids Wales.

793 Vikings raid Lindisfarne Island and its monastery off the Northumbrian coast. This marks the beginning of Viking raids on Anglo-Saxon England.

796 Offa of Mercia dies.

865 A Danish Viking army invades Wessex. There are battles at Reading, Ashdown, Basing and Meretun.

871 Alfred becomes king of Wessex. He fights the Vikings at Wilton and elsewhere. The West Saxons make peace with the Vikings, buying them off with money.

871/2 Vikings camp in London for the winter. The Mercians make peace with the Vikings, buying them off with money.

872/3 Vikings invade Northumbria.

874/5 Alfred wins a naval battle against the Vikings.

875 The monks of Lindisfarne abandon their monastery because of the repeated Viking raids.

876 Vikings move to Dorset, and Alfred makes peace with the Vikings.

876 Vikings share out the land of the Northumbrians among the army.

876/7 Vikings reach as far west as Exeter.

877 Vikings take over eastern Mercia.

878 By this date, Vikings have taken over all Anglo-Saxon lands. Alfred is forced to hide in the marshes.

878 Later that year, at the Battle of Edington, Alfred defeats Guthrum's army and Guthrum becomes a Christian.

879/
880 Guthrum's army shares out the land of East Anglia.

880 Aethelred becomes king of Mercia, but the land is now under the control of Alfred of Wessex.

882 Alfred wins a naval battle against the Vikings.

885 Alfred raids East Anglia.

886 Alfred occupies London.

896 Many Vikings give up their raids on Anglo-Saxon lands.

899 Death of King Alfred.

978 Aethelred II (also known as Ethelred) becomes king of England.

980 Viking raids resume, this time on southern England, using Normandy (France) as a base. Vikings paid off in gold.

1002 Aethelred marries Emma of Normandy.

1003 Sweyn, the king of Denmark, and his army seize Exeter, then return to sea.

1013 Sweyn returns, drives out Aethelred and takes over as king of England. Aethelred escapes to Normandy.

1014 Sweyn dies and his son, Canute, becomes king. However, Aethelred returns and drives out the Vikings.

1016 Aethelred dies, and England is overrun by the Vikings. Canute becomes king of England again.

-1035 Death of Canute.

-1042 Edward (the Confessor) becomes king of England.

-1066 Edward dies. Harold Godwinsson becomes the last Anglo-Saxon king of England. He is defeated by William of Normandy, at the Battle of Hastings.

Words and names

ALFRED (KING 871–900) The youngest son of King Aethelwulf of Wessex. Alfred became king of Wessex during a time of Viking attack. At first he was defeated but was later victorious against the Danish King Guthrum, defeating him at the Battle of Edington.

Alfred created a network of defensive towns, or burhs, started a navy, made a written code of law and supported the arts. For all his achievements, he has become known as Alfred the Great.

ANCESTOR People belonging to a previous generation.

ANGLES One of the Germanic peoples who, along with the Jutes and Saxons, invaded England in the fifth century AD. The Angles gave their name to England.

ANGLO-SAXON CHRONICLES A series of books written during Anglo-Saxon times and thought to have been begun by King Alfred in about AD 890. They give a good, if one-sided, account of history through the time of the Viking invasions.

ANGLO-SAXONS The peoples who invaded England from the fifth century from areas that are now southern Denmark, Germany and The Netherlands.

ARCHAEOLOGY The study of the past by digging up and examining the remains of buildings and artefacts such as pottery, jewellery and tools.

ARMOUR Gear made for people to help protect them during battle.

BATTLE OF HASTINGS The battle of 14 October 1066 in which the forces of Duke William of Normandy met the forces of King Harold of England on a hill near to the southern town of Hastings. The events leading up to the battle as far as the crowning of William are shown by the Bayeux Tapestry.

BEDE (673–735) Often known as the Venerable Bede, Bede was the author of a book called *The Ecclesiastical History of the English People* which he completed in AD 731. This work is our primary source for understanding the beginnings of the English people and the coming of Christianity. This is the first work of history in which the AD dating system is used.

BRITISH The Celtic people who lived in Britain at the time of the Roman invasion. During Anglo-Saxon times, many of the British became slaves; others fled to remote regions in the west of the country, to Wales, Devon and Cornwall.

BURH A fort planned by Alfred as a way of offering safe haven against the Danes. Each burh became a market centre and also a seat of local government.

CEORL The ceorl was the freeman farmer in Anglo-Saxon society. He farmed land for a nobleman and paid a rent in food (called *feorm*, from which we get the word 'farm'). Although he was not one of the warrior nobles, all able-bodied freemen could be called upon to bear arms in defence of the tribe's homelands.

CHIEFTAIN The leader of a small group of people.

DANELAW The region of Danish influence in the time of Alfred the Great. It occupied much of eastern England.

EOLDERMAN A senior noble (thane) and landowner who looked after a shire or group of shires for the king. The word was later changed to eorl.

FREEMAN Someone who was not a slave and did not belong to another person.

FYRD An army raised from the people of a shire when there was danger of attack.

GRAVE GOODS The items buried with a person. The Anglo-Saxons, along with many other pagan peoples, thought that clothes, swords and other items were needed for the afterlife.

HIDE In Anglo-Saxon times the amount of land needed to feed a freeman family. In Norman times a hide was equal to about 120 acres (50 hectares) of farmland, but in Anglo-Saxon times was probably much less.

HILL FORT A defensive site on a hill top and surrounded by earthen banks. These features were built by the British in the centuries before the Romans invaded.

HUNDRED A part of an English shire made up of one hundred hides.

JUTES A Germanic people who, along with the Angles and Saxons, invaded Britain in the fifth century AD. According to Bede, they settled in Kent, parts of Hampshire and on the Isle of Wight.

LATIN The language of the ancient Romans; it continued to be used by the church and in books after the collapse of the Roman empire.

LINDISFARNE GOSPELS The most important surviving treasure from early Northumbria. Written between 715 and 720 in honour of St Cuthbert, Bishop of Lindisfarne. The manuscript was made in the monastery of Lindisfarne, on Holy Island, off the coast of modern-day Northumberland.

MERCIA One of the most powerful of the early English kingdoms, Mercia occupied much of what is today the Midlands. It was originally settled by Angles. It was destroyed by the Viking arrivals of 872. After this Mercia was ruled only by an eolderman.

MISSIONARY People belonging to a church who arrive in a land in order to convert people to their faith.

NORMANS The people from Normandy in France. They were descended from Vikings but spoke a form of French.

NORTHUMBRIA One of the main kingdoms of early England, Northumbria covered what is today the north of England. It was originally settled by the Angles and became the most powerful kingdom in the seventh century. Thereafter it was less powerful as first the kings of Mercia, then Wessex, became the most powerful rulers.

OFFA (KING 757-796) Powerful king of Mercia during the eighth century. Offa took power in Mercia by murdering his cousin. By fighting his neighbours, he added more and more land until Mercia was the most powerful of the Anglo-Saxon kingdoms. His territory stretched from the River Humber to London. Offa was the first English ruler to mint the silver penny and the first to stamp his name on his coins. He was known as "king of the English".

PAGAN In Anglo-Saxon times, a person who worships non-Christian gods.

POPE The leader of the church who lived in Rome.

ROMANS The warrior people who were based in Rome (now in modern Italy) and who conquered a large part of Europe, North Africa and the Near East about 2,000 years ago. They conquered Britain in AD 43, but left when the empire became weak about AD 410.

SAXONS One of the Germanic peoples (from Saxony) who, along with the Angles and Jutes, invaded England in the fifth century and who mainly occupied the south and south west of England.

SHIRE A group of hundreds which made up an area about the size of a modern county. They were the largest areas in a kingdom.

SLAVE A person who is not free and is bought and sold.

SUTTON HOO A place in Suffolk where a spectacular Anglo-Saxon grave was found in 1938. It was found not to have been robbed and yielded spectacular evidence of the burial of an important king.

THANE/THEGN Thanes were warriors who protected the king as bodyguards.

THRALL A slave in Anglo-Saxon England. However, thralls could earn money and own property. If they earned enough money, they could buy their own freedom.

TRIBE A group of people who live in one part of a country and are ruled by a chieftain.

VALHALLA In pagan Anglo-Saxon belief, a place where warriors killed in battle would go.

VIKINGS The people of Denmark, Sweden and Norway who raided and invaded much of northern Europe during the eighth to eleventh centuries. They settled in eastern England and controlled an area called the Danelaw.

WAR LORD A chieftain who remained in power by means of force rather than from the popular support of his people.

WARRIOR A person whose main job was to fight in battle. Anglo-Saxon warriors were thanes.

WESSEX An early English kingdom occupying southern and south-western England, but not including Devon and Cornwall. Their rulers rose to become the most important kings in England in the ninth century. Alfred the Great was a king of Wessex.

WITAN A council which advised an Anglo-Saxon king. Its members included bishops and the most important nobles.

Index